i

Contents

Abstract

The counter-piracy efforts off the coast of Somalia currently consist of three international operations and several unilaterally deployed naval assets. Coordination, primarily through infrequent meetings, is the means by which these forces attempt to achieve unity of effort. Such a method is not consistent with military doctrine and results in a disorganized and inefficient operation. This paper illustrates how achieving unity of effort through unity of command will benefit the counter-piracy mission. It explains how consolidation of forces under the direction of a single operational commander will increase the efficiency of counter-piracy operations off the coast of Somalia by improving communication and coordination, balancing time, space and force, and by keeping the operation focused at a constabulary effort. Finally, the paper offers recommendations that allow for inclusion of all international forces into a single counter-piracy maritime police force and how the existing coordination avenues can continue to provide valuable communications.

The seriousness of piracy was recently brought home to many Americans by the murder of a four-person crew sailing through the Indian Ocean in February 2011, less than a year after the tense rescue of the crew of the Maersk Alabama cargo ship. Prior to these attacks, most Americans were likely to associate a pirate with Hollywood's mascara-wearing Johnny Depp rather than a young man from eastern Africa. Despite the perception that piracy was a nineteenth century problem, it continues to threaten the security of maritime trade every bit as much as in the days of wooden sailing ships and Aztec gold. In light of the recent murder, pirates are just as violent. While pirates are no longer associated with eye patches and wooden legs, their overall goal is very much the same: to achieve financial gain by intercepting merchant shipping. The financial gain these days is in the form of ransom rather than the seizure of precious cargo. The United Nations (UN) has recognized piracy as an international criminal activity and it has called upon all nations to repress this criminal enterprise. In response, several nations have provided naval forces, either independently or in a coalition, with the goal of protecting merchant shipping from piracy. The past several years have seen a startling increase in the number of pirate attacks in the waters around Somalia. The international response to this particular area has been significant and has resulted in a reduction of successful pirate attacks, especially within the Gulf of Aden. However, the approach to countering Somali pirates is disorganized. The international community attempts to achieve unity of effort by relying heavily on the coordination of these naval forces. The effectiveness of currently deployed forces could be improved drastically by simply reorganizing them to achieve unity of command. To improve the efficiency of counter-piracy operations near Somalia, the naval forces there should be organized under a single operational commander to achieve unity of effort.

The Counter-Piracy Model vs. Military Doctrine:

The United Nations Convention on the Law of the Sea (UNCLOS) generally defines piracy as any illegal acts of violence, detention or depredation, committed for private ends by the crew of a private ship or aircraft either on the high seas or outside of the jurisdiction of any State as well as participation in, or facilitation of, those acts. [1] Piracy threatens maritime security around the globe in places like the Strait of Malacca near Indonesia, the Gulf of Aden near Somalia and Africa's western coast. While piracy still poses a threat wherever there is substantial commercial maritime traffic, pirate activity is particularly rampant in the waters off the coast of Somalia. The threat in this region ranges geographically from the Gulf of Aden in the north and the Indian Ocean in the east. These waters are a prime operating area for pirates for a number of reasons. The Gulf of Aden is one of the world's busiest commercial shipping routes. Twenty thousand to thirty thousand vessels transit the area each year, representing one tenth of world trade.[2] Somalia is an economically depressed country with few jobs and extreme poverty, which provides an appealing financial incentive for piracy as a means of income. Somalia also lacks a stable government. The Transitional Federal Government (TFG) is the internationally recognized sovereign authority of Somalia, but the country is actually divided into three semi-autonomous regions. To complicate the regional division, the TFG has only marginal capacity to influence the limited area around the capital city of Mogadishu. There are no real means to uphold the rule of law throughout Somalia, which effectively provides a haven for criminal organizations to orchestrate attacks with impunity.

It is widely recognized that the overall solution to piracy in these waters is to stabilize Somalia, thereby removing the economic incentive and legal void. To some, a military approach to repress piracy appears as a Band-Aid on a much larger wound; however, it should not be completely ruled out as part of the solution. Certainly there is a necessity to provide for the immediate physical security of merchant shipping until the strategic goal of a stabilized Somalia can be achieved. Furthermore, there is a legitimate historical precedent for such a response. For instance, the U.S. Navy has its origins in counter-piracy along the Barbary Coast. The UN has also established international legitimacy for military operations against pirates through the UNCLOS and several UN Security Council Resolutions (UNSCRs). The UNCLOS, in addition to defining piracy, calls upon all states to "cooperate to the fullest possible extent in the repression of piracy on the high seas or in any other place outside the jurisdiction of any State."[3] Additionally, since 2008, there have been eight UNSCRs providing authority for an international military response.

While the UN calls for maximum cooperation, it provides little guidance on how that cooperation should be obtained. Current counter-piracy operations off the coast of Somalia "now include EU's operation Atalanta, NATO's Operation Ocean Shield, [and] the US Combined Task Force 151 [CTF 151]."[4] Additionally, naval forces and aircraft are independently deployed to the region from China, India, Iran, Japan, Malaysia, the Republic of Korea, Russia, Saudi Arabia and Yemen.[5]

A brief discussion of military doctrine will help in understanding how militaries, such as those listed above, can successfully accomplish their mission. Unity of effort is the principle of war that ensures all available resources are being used in concert to achieve a given objective. Without unity of effort, orchestrated at the operational level of war, subordinate tactical actions risk becoming random and disorganized. Dr. Milan Vego, author of *Joint Operational Warfare Theory and Practice*, identifies unity of effort as a major requirement for any successful operation and acknowledges that it is accomplished either through unity of command or cooperation.[6] "Normally, the highest degree of effectiveness is ensured by having unity of effort through unity of command."[7] Reinforcing Dr. Vego's assertion, US Joint Military Doctrine *Multinational Operations* recognizes coordination as generally inferior to unity of command. The doctrine recommends coordination be reserved for planning and the use of coordination in actual operations be limited as much as practical.[8] Military doctrine, based on the study of centuries of warfare, concludes that unity of effort is best achieved through unity of command. The lack of a single operational commander contradicts this concept. Inadequate development of command and control (C2) is often a contributing factor whenever a military operation fails to accomplish an objective smoothly and quickly. While not synonymous with unity of command, C2 is closely related and is equally important. C2 is the means by which a commander communicates and issues orders among his forces. Properly developed C2 requires that a clear relationship exists between senior and subordinate forces. Without unity of command, the C2 structure becomes complex and confusing. Often subordinate forces receive orders that are redundant or conflicting or they are inconsistent with the objectives. Thus, without unity of command and a clearly defined C2 structure, it becomes exceedingly difficult to achieve unity of effort.

The Case for the Status Quo:

Some would argue that there is no need for unity of command because current counter-piracy efforts have been, and will likely continue to be successful without it. Critics of a single operational commander are quick to acknowledge that recent success has proven current efforts are sufficient to repress piracy around Somalia and the naval forces have created "an Internationally Recognised Transit Corridor, providing safe passage to vessels in the Gulf of Aden."[9] Additionally, The Contact Group on Piracy off the Coast of Somalia was established in response to UNSCR 1851 to ensure international coordination of antipiracy activities.[10] It is a strategic-level partnership of over 50 countries that works to addresses all aspects of countering piracy including coordination of military forces, judicial issues, strengthening merchant shipping protection awareness and public information.[11] Tom Countryman, the Principal Deputy Assistant Secretary for Political Military Affairs, led a U.S. delegation to the Contact Group meeting on January 28, 2010. In a brief concerning that meeting, he addressed the coordination efforts between the various nations conducting counter-piracy as "a good model not only for the Gulf of Aden and the Somali bases, but also for future such endeavors."[12] Mr. Countryman championed this success despite a "need for there to be a supreme commander in charge of the effort."[13] By these assertions, Mr. Countryman defies military doctrine and advocates for a precariously loose military command structure.

While Mr. Countryman views his counter-piracy model as the way of the future, some argue that a successful model already exists in the form used to combat piracy in the Strait of Malacca. These advocates claim that the same practices employed in the Strait would achieve similar success if applied toward Somalia. Indeed, there are similarities between the two regions. Like the Gulf of Aden, commercial traffic through the Strait of Malacca represents a substantial part of world trade. Additionally, the geography of the Gulf of Aden and the Strait of Malacca make merchant shipping an easy target for pirates. Piracy in the Strait of Malacca reached a peak in 2004, with thirty-eight attacks, but had dwindled to just two attacks by 2008.[14] Such dramatic success provides a glimmer for cautious optimism with regard to Somalia. Some experts have suggested that transplanting this approach to east Africa is the appropriate course of action.[15] However, stark differences between the two situations mean that simply applying the same techniques from the Strait of Malacca to the Somali coast will not yield instant success.

Unity of Command Improves Coordination and Communication:

When compared to either The Contact Group or the Strait of Malacca model, unity of command is superior because of the efficiency it offers to accomplish the mission. Unity of command will improve efficiency because a single operational commander can more effectively communicate and coordinate forces within the rigid structure of a single chain of command. Unity of command improves communication by providing the operational commander with a reliable means to disseminate timely lessons-learned and best practices among his forces. Such information is essential to adapt quickly to an evolving piracy threat. Additionally, unity of command ensures that first-hand knowledge of the operating environment is not lost as ships and aircraft rotate through the theater. Unity of command improves coordination by allowing a single operational commander to redistribute his forces within the operational area in response to a dynamic threat.

Significant differences between Somalia and the Strait of Malacca mean that a counter-piracy model is not immediately transferable. In the Strait of Malacca, the forces were mostly provided by the regional countries of Malaysia, Singapore and Indonesia. Initially, these countries lacked robust international cooperation and attempted to address the pirate threat unilaterally. In the face of a crisis-level threat, the countries were forced to work together more closely, going so far as providing mixed-nationality aircrews to conduct surveillance flights.[16] Neither these regional nations, nor those that provided assistance, ever established unity of command under a single operational commander. Instead, they relied solely on coordination efforts such as the Regional Agreement on Combating Piracy and Armed Robbery (ReCAAP) which "established an organization that operates an advanced information fusion and sharing center in Singapore."[17] Such a coordination-centric model was successful in the Strait of Malacca for a number of reasons, including the political stability of the regional nations. From a C2 perspective, the model was only successful due to the relative ease with which so few nations can coordinate and communicate. Despite the ability to achieve unity of effort without establishing a single operational commander, this example should be seen as the exception rather than the rule. In contrast to the Strait of Malacca, there are many more nations involved in the counter-piracy effort near Somalia. Reliance on coordination alone with such a large and diverse group of nations is insufficient to achieve unity of effort.

Efforts to develop an information-sharing center for Somalia similar to that in Singapore have been attempted, but the same level of coordination has not been achieved. The Contact Group is divided into four different Working Groups, each assigned a subject area to support reaching its overall strategic goals. Working Group 1, concerned with the international naval effort, is chaired by the United Kingdom and focuses on "force generation, operational coordination and capacity-building."[18] Another avenue through which nations attempt to coordinate information sharing is the Shared Awareness and Deconfliction (SHADE) program, which meets at the headquarters of the US FIFTH Fleet in Bahrain.[19] While these two organizations work closely together, the fact that there are two organizations attempting to replicate the success of the Singapore information center demonstrates the difficulty inherent in coordination between such a diverse group of nations. Furthermore, these organizations meet infrequently: Working Group 1 meets, on average, twice a year while SHADE meetings are conducted monthly. These infrequent meetings are not sufficient to coordinate employment of forces during day-to-day operations and, therefore, are not a suitable replacement for unity of command.

Although the naval forces operating near Somalia are diverse, they still have a lot in common. They all derive their authority to conduct counter-piracy operations from the same UNSCRs and UNCLOS. Many of these nations also share common alliances. Nine countries participate in all three major international operations: NATO's OPERATION OCEAN SHIELD, the EU's OPERATION ATALANTA and CTF 151. Several more countries contribute to at least two of these international operations. Counter-piracy forces all have similar objectives, as well. For instance, the EU's OPERATION ATALANTA is meant to "provide protection for vessels chartered by the WFP [World Food Program] [and] provide protection for merchant vessels."[20] NATO's OPERATION OCEAN SHIELD "will aim to assist regional states, upon their request, in developing their own ability to combat piracy activities."[21] These efforts, while more specific, are nested within the overall objective of repressing piracy: an objective shared by all international operations. With so much in common, the presence of three different international operations is disorganized and wasteful. Such an approach is counter to military doctrine concerning unity of command. By consolidation of these forces, a single operational commander could streamline his efforts to accomplish the objective.

Of course with the diversity among the nations operating near Somalia, some might be hesitant to commit their naval forces to a unified command structure, especially if it is western-led. China, Iran and Yemen come to mind. Dr. Vego points out that unity of effort is often achieved through cooperation in coalition warfare.[22] However, he also recognizes that "optimally, a single theater commander should be appointed, with authority and responsibility over all the subordinate multinational force of all services."[23] Due to unique circumstances in every theater, total unity of command is rare. Working Group 1 and SHADE provide a useful avenue to coordinate the main coalition effort with those nations reluctant to join, but they should not be seen as an effective replacement for unity of command. The difficulty in achieving unity of command does not diminish the importance of consolidating the command structure as much as the situation will allow. Nor should the difficulty in achieving unity of command outweigh the benefit of increased efficiency toward accomplishing the objective. While the reality of international politics may hinder the achievement of 100 percent unity of command, consolidation of as many forces as practical into a coherent command structure would significantly improve efficiency.

Unity of Command and the Factors of Time, Space, and Force

In addition to improving coordination and communication, unity of command will improve the efficiency with which an operational commander employs forces with regard to space and time. The importance of balancing the resources of time, space, and force cannot be overemphasized. An improper balance increases the risk of mission failure either from the excessive or insufficient employment of forces in a given geographic location or the inability to react to a given threat in a timely manner. Through unity of command, a single operational commander can redistribute his forces in order to mitigate this risk.

An example of how an operational commander can adjust the balance of force and space is evident through examination of the expanded geographic area threatened by pirates.

When Mr. Countryman refers to success by the current counter-piracy forces, his comment limits these victories geographically to the narrow passage of the Gulf of Aden. Furthermore, his comment only reflects the decrease in the number of successful attacks. Certainly the presence of naval forces has had a positive impact toward repressing piracy. This is analogous to the way a policeman, by parking his car on the median of a busy highway, will reduce the number of speeding violations. In his statement, Mr. Countryman fails to recognize that the overall number of attempted attacks has increased or that those attacks have spread further south along the eastern coast of Africa.[24] It is not surprising that pirate attacks would continue outside the geographical limits of the Gulf of Aden. Just as the presence of a police car reduces speeding violations, motorists are likely to continue speeding once they feel they are comfortably past the reach of the radar gun. Similarly, as international patrols thwarted successful pirate attacks, the pirates have evolved their tactics to attack where the patrols lack a presence. A similar phenomenon occurred in Afghanistan and Iraq. There too, initial success was a double-edged sword. Insurgents in these countries were pushed into more remote locations as coalition forces routed them from key cities. Counter-piracy forces have done the same thing with the Gulf of Aden. In Afghanistan and Iraq, a temporary increase in troops, commonly known as the surge, allowed coalition forces to increase pressure on insurgents while maintaining their influence in key cities. Since forces are already stretched thin by ongoing operations around the Middle East, it is unlikely that counter-piracy efforts will receive a similar surge of naval assets. Therefore, the fragile gains made in the Gulf of Aden are in danger of reversal if the currently deployed forces attempt to confront the expanded threat without first achieving unity of command.

To meet this expanded threat efficiently, there are a number of options available to an operational commander. One example is to build upon the success in the Gulf of Aden by expanding the Internationally Recommended Transit Corridor (IRTC). Since February 2009, the IRTC has allowed naval and air assets to patrol the area in the best way to protect and support merchant shipping.[25] The IRTC is essentially a traffic scheme for merchant shipping that allows the naval forces to concentrate their efforts over a reduced space in order to offer an umbrella of collective protection. By extending this scheme further off the coast of Africa and the Arabian Peninsula, an operational commander could dramatically narrow the area of the ocean he needs to patrol, thereby improving the balance of force and space. Other examples include establishing a "tailored maritime exclusion zone" and using unmanned systems for surveillance.[26] The "tailored exclusion zone" would allow an operational commander to enforce prohibition on certain piracy related equipment which are not normally associated with fishing, such as high-horsepower motors, automatic weapons and rocket-propelled grenades.[27] Unmanned systems offer an improvement in force when compared with the number of personnel required to operate a maritime patrol aircraft. However, unmanned systems are in high demand in other theaters which limits their availability. These examples are merely options available to balance the limited forces over a broad space, and there are certainly more than just these three options. The key is that any option is of little value without unity of command. A single operational commander, through his years of experience and familiarity with the operational environment, is required to ensure that the right option, or combination of options, is employed to maximize the balance of force and space.

Just as important as the balance of force and space is the balance between force and time. Every summer there is a seasonal increase of wind in the Indian Ocean, known as the monsoon. As these winds build speed over the vast ocean surface, the seas further from shore become treacherous for the types of small boats employed by pirates. There is a recognized correlation between the monsoon and the frequency of pirate attacks.[28] The piracy rate generally decreases during the monsoons. Furthermore, attacks are conducted closer to the Somali coast or one of the larger "mother ships" that pirates use as a mobile base of operations. A single operational commander could take advantage of this environmental shift by adjusting the deployment schedules of his ships and concentrating his forces to match the likelihood of an attack.

Constraining Operations to a Constabulary Effort:

In addition to improving the efficiency of counter-piracy forces, unity of command will ensure the focus of operations remains on the appropriate level of the spectrum of conflict. Since UNCLOS defines piracy as an illegal act done by a private entity, it should be considered a crime and not an act of war. The appropriate level on the spectrum of conflict is a police action. The concept of constraining operations to a constabulary effort is important because of the complexity of the legal landscape. Since a merchant vessel can be owned by the interests of one nation, flagged in a second nation, and crewed by persons from a third nation, suspected pirates lie in a web of overlapping legal jurisdiction. There are a number of issues involved with the prosecution of pirates. Most of these lie well beyond the responsibility of the operational commander; however, counter-piracy operations can substantially complicate these issues. For instance, the collection of evidence is something done at the scene of the pirate attack that could impede forthcoming prosecutions. The current disorganized international approach to repress piracy means there are more opportunities to overlook details and mishandle evidence. A single operational commander could employ his military forces while maintaining the focus on a constabulary mission in order to support the overall legal effort. Consolidation of forces into a coherent command structure is the most effective way of ensuring that detained pirates do not slip through the cracks of an international legal system.

A single operational commander would be more effective at presenting a consistent law enforcement effort than the current international approach. While some nations have successfully brought Somali pirates to justice through domestic legal processes, others have deployed their naval forces to the region without the authority to detain suspected pirates.[29] Additionally, some states "released captured pirates unpunished due to legal and diplomatic confusion or difficulty in detaining and prosecuting the perpetrators in criminal court."[30] This practice sends mixed messages to would-be pirates and substantially hinders the deterrent effect of counter-piracy operations.

Unity of command would improve the deterrence effect of counter-piracy forces by presenting a consistent constabulary presence. A single operational commander could draw upon the law enforcement expertise inherent in the participating nations. By the nature of their size, the naval forces of many smaller nations involved in counter-piracy are proficient with enforcing maritime law. For those forces, law enforcement is a routine duty in their own national waters. In contrast, the US Navy lacks this inherent expertise and authority due to decades of focus on military operations against other state actors and domestic law enforcement limitations imposed by the Posse Comitatus Act. The US Coast Guard, on the other hand, is very proficient at, and has the authority for maritime law enforcement.

Successful counter-drug operations in South America are a result of merging the capabilities of these two forces, by augmenting US Navy ships with US Coast Guard law enforcement detachments (LEDETs). Similarly, CTF 151 employs the US Coast Guard primarily "to provide training in evidence collection practices and procedures to ensure a complete case package, which facilitates prosecution."[31] Due to limited availability and increasing responsibility at home, the US Coast Guard cannot afford to commit additional assets to support counter-piracy efforts. An operational commander would be in a position to ensure that the diverse law enforcement expertise brought by each nation is utilized in the most efficient manner.

More than just efficiency, the operational commander has another reason to limit operations to a lower part of the spectrum of conflict. He needs to refrain from escalating hostilities by pirates. A solution that is often suggested as a defensive practice is to employ private security details aboard merchant vessels. On the surface, this suggestion seems to have some merit. Certainly armed security guards would be able to defend their ship from marauders in small boats. However, most experts discourage this practice due to fear that it will cause pirates to resort to ever more dangerous attempts to seize a ship. By the same rationale, US counter-piracy efforts should likewise seek to limit the escalation of force. The current model allows room for independent nations to act aggressively toward a suspected pirate. Such a unilateral response would be counter-productive toward limiting the escalation of hostilities. A single operational commander would be responsible for the conduct of those under his charge and would be able to ensure that all forces were on the same sheet of music with regard to the best amount of force to use.

The most effective means for an operational commander to limit the use of force and keep the focus on a constabulary level is through the development of common rules of engagement (ROE). Each international counter-piracy operation has a defined ROE and each independently deployed nation uses its national ROE. The distinction is that the ROE is neither common between the different operations nor among the independently deployed naval forces. Common ROE among a coalition, while not a new concept, can be very difficult to establish. To be effective, the ROE must balance political concerns, the international legal obligations of participating countries and the military operational objectives. The political and legal issues cannot be addressed easily because they are much broader than just repressing piracy. This will certainly lead to national caveats that will limit exactly what each nation's force can do. This is the reality of multinational operations. However, the third consideration of military operational objectives can be consolidated easily if there is agreement upon those objectives. Establishment of a single operational commander is a better means to ensure all objectives are aligned, especially when the alternative is reliance on Working Group 1 or SHADE. Therefore, unity of command is the surest way to establish common ROE among all counter-piracy forces.

The Way Ahead

To achieve the required unity of command, the UN should issue a resolution calling for all nations conducting counter-piracy operations to be consolidated into a single operation under the UN flag. While there are plenty of precedents for UN peacekeeping and stability operations ashore, there has never been a UN maritime police force. The current situation in the waters surrounding Somalia represents a perfect opportunity to implement such a force. While the pursuit of suspected pirates into Somali territorial waters is approved under

15

UNSCR, the counter-piracy force typically operates in international waters. Since a country's territorial sovereignty is not threatened, there should be little resistance in forming the maritime police force. Additionally, operations conducted under the UN flag lend a higher level of legitimacy to the efforts and provide a means to redress differences between participating nations. Also, every nation has a vested interest in the security of maritime trade. A mission under the UN flag would allow piracy to be repressed without undue burden on any one nation in pursuit of a goal that benefits all. Of course, this UN maritime police force would be more useful if it were coupled with a UN sanctioned criminal court that could address the legal prosecution of suspected pirates. If successful, the maritime police force could be a model for counter-piracy efforts conducted anywhere around the globe.

Another useful model is the work being done by the Contact Group. While their coordination is insufficient to influence day-to-day operations, they have made significant progress toward international cooperation. The operational commander should incorporate the Contact Group into his coordination and communication capability. It would provide a means to develop and maintain a database of lessons-learned, best practices and the identities of suspected pirates. It could also be the conduit to communicate this information throughout the maritime police force. Additionally, the Contact Group can act as a bridge between the maritime police force and merchant shipping to increase the commercial vessel's awareness of likely pirate locations. Furthermore, they can continue to educate merchant mariners on recommended defensive measure as well as coordinate group transit through areas of increased threat.

Conclusion:

While international efforts have improved maritime security off the coast of Somalia, piracy remains a significant and growing threat to international commerce and marine safety. Significant pirate activity has been successfully repressed in South Asia by the close cooperation of regional nations, but parallels between the Strait of Malacca and Somalia are limited. Simply transplanting the same principles to Somalia will be insufficient to address the pirate threat there. The threat of piracy will not be fully eradicated until Somalia is stabilized sufficiently to reduce the economic incentive and legal impunity that makes piracy appealing. However, this is a strategic solution that will require more than military efforts and will take many years to achieve. In the meantime, reorganization of the naval forces currently conducting counter-piracy operations will improve efficiency. To achieve unity of effort, these forces should be consolidated under a single operational commander. Unity of command will reduce reliance on the complex coordination efforts of the Contact Group and SHADE to orchestrate daily tasks and will facilitate communication throughout a rigid chain of command. Unity of command also allows the operational commander to adjust his forces within the region to reduce redundancies in coverage area and react to an attack in a timely manner with just the right amount of force. Finally, unity of command will allow the operational commander to ensure that counter-piracy efforts are constrained to a constabulary action to provide a consistent law enforcement deterrence and to ensure successful prosecution of suspected pirates.

End Notes

———————————

[1] United Nations, *The United Nations Convention on the Law of the Sea*, 61.

[2] Merle David Kellerhals Jr., "U.S. Charges 11 Somalis."

[3] United Nations, *The United Nations Convention on the Law of the Sea*, 60.

[4] United Nations, "Somalia: Piracy," 2.

[5] United Nations, "The Situation in Somalia," S/Res/1950.

[6] Milan N. Vego, *Joint Operational Warfare*, VIII-13.

[7] Ibid.

[8] Chairman, U.S. Joint Chiefs of Staff, *Multinational Operations*, II-5.

[9] United Nations, "Somalia: Piracy," 2.

[10] Ibid.

[11] Ibid.

[12] Tom Countryman, "Update Briefing."

[13] Ibid.

[14] Michael Schuman, "How to Defeat Pirates."

[15] James Kraska, "Fresh Thinking," 147.

[16] Michael Schuman, "How to Defeat Pirates."

[17] James Kraska, "Fresh Thinking," 146.

[18] U.S. Department of State, "International Response."

[19] U.S. Department of State, "Seventh Plenary Meeting."

[20] European Union, "EU naval operation."

[21] North Atlantic Treaty Organization, "Operation Ocean Shield."

[22] Milan N. Vego, *Joint Operational Warfare*, VIII-16

[23] Ibid., VIII-17

[24] Merle David Kellerhals Jr., "U.S. Charges 11 Somalis."

[25] International Chamber of Commerce, "Piracy Prone Areas."

[26] James Kraska, "Fresh Thinking," 149-150.

[27] Ibid.

[28] Mike Pflanz, "Somali Pirate Attacks."

[29] James Kraska, "Fresh Thinking," 144.

[30] Ibid.

[31] Tony Migliorini, "Coast Guard Contributes."

Bibliography

Countryman, Tom. "Update Briefing on Anti-Piracy Efforts." U.S. Department of State, Washington, DC, 18 February 2010. http://www.africom.mil/printStory.asp?art=4052 (accessed 22 February 2011).

European Union. Common Security and Defense Policy. "EU naval operation against piracy (EUNAVFOR Somalia – Operation ATALANTA)." http://www.consilium.europa.eu/ showPage.aspx?id=1521&lang=en (accessed 23 February 2011).

International Chamber of Commerce. "Piracy Prone Areas and Warnings." http://www.icc-ccs.org/home/piracy-reporting-centre/prone-areas-and-warnings (accessed 05 April 2011).

Kellerhals Jr., Merle David. "U.S. Charges 11 Somalis with Maritime Piracy." America.gov, 29 April 2010. http://www.africom.mil/printStory.asp?art=4334 (accessed 22 February 2011).

Kraska, James. "Fresh Thinking For An Old Problem: Report of the Naval War College Workshop on Countering Maritime Piracy." *Naval War College Review* 62, no. 4 (Autumn 2009) 141-154.

Migliorini, Tony. "Coast Guard Contributes to Counter-piracy Mission." Coast Guard Headquarters Public Affairs, 24 February 2009. http://www.africom.mil/ printStory.asp?art=2733 (accessed on 22 February 2011).

North Atlantic Treaty Organization. "Operation Ocean Shield Current News." http://www.manw.nato.int/page_operation_ocean_shield.aspx (accessed 18 April 2011).

Pflanz, Mike. "Somali pirate attacks 'set to increase' as monsoon eases." The Telegraph, 27 July 2009. http://www.telegraph.co.uk/news/worldnews/africaandindianocean/somalia/591890 8/Somali-pirate-attacks-set-to-increase-as-monsoon-eases.html (accessed 30 March 2011).

Schuman, Michael. "How to Defeat Pirates: Success in the Strait." *Time*, 22 April 2009. http://www.time.com/time/printout/0,8816,1893032,00.html# (accessed 09 Apr 2011).

United Nations. Security Council. "Somalia: Piracy." Security Council Report Update Report No. 3. New York: UN, 2006. http://www.securitycouncilreport.org/atf/cf/% 7B65BFCF9B-6D27-4E9C-8CD3-CF6E4FF96FF9%7D/Update%20Report%2020% 20April%2010_Somalia.pdf (accessed 23 February 2011).

————. Security Council. "The situation in Somalia." S/Res/1950. 2010. http://www.un.org/Docs/sc/unsc_resolutions10.htm (accessed 29 May 2010).

————. *The United Nations Convention on the Law of the Sea.* Montego Bay, Jamaica,1982. http://www.un.org/Depts/los/convention_agreements/convention_overview_ convention.htm (accessed 29 May 2011).

U.S. Department of State. "International Response." Diplomacy in Action. http://www.state.gov/t/pm/ppa/piracy/contactgroup/index.htm (accessed 23 February 2011).

————. "Seventh Plenary Meeting of the Contact Group on Piracy off the coast of Somalia." Diplomacy in Action. http://www.state.gov/t/pm/rls/othr/misc/151795.htm (accessed 23   February 2011).

U.S. Office of the Chairman of the Joint Chiefs of Staff. *Multinational Operations.* Joint Publication (JP) 3-16. Washington, DC: CJCS, 07 March 2007.

Vego, Milan N. *Joint Operational Warfare Theory and Practice.* 2007. Reprint, Newport, RI: U.S. Naval War College, 2009.

www.ingramcontent.com/pod-product-compliance
Lightning Source LLC
Chambersburg PA
CBHW081251170526
45165CB00009B/3282